WHAT IS CULTURE?

Bobbie Kalman

Crabtree Publishing Company

www.crabtreebooks.com

Our Multicultural World

Created by
Bobbie Kalman

Inspired by my experiences as a refugee and immigrant, my extensive travels, my wonderful students in Nassau and Germany, and my amazing ESL classes at Forest Manor P.S.

Author and Editor-in-Chief
Bobbie Kalman

Editor
Kathy Middleton

Proofreader
Crystal Sikkens

Photo research
Bobbie Kalman

Design
Bobbie Kalman
Katherine Berti
Samantha Crabtree (cover)

Production coordinator
Katherine Berti

Illustrations
William Band: page 1 (right symbols)
Barbara Bedell: page 1 (presents)
Katherine Berti: page 6
Antoinette "Cookie" Bortolon: page 1 (fish)
Brenda Clark: page 5 (bottom right)
Rose Gowsell: page 1 (top dragon)
Bonna Rouse: pages 1 (bottom dragon, left symbol, and soccer ball), 22, 23
Margaret Amy Salter: page 8 (top)

Photographs
Marc Crabtree: pages 17 (bottom right), 23 (bottom left)
Dreamstime.com: page 19 (bottom)
iStockphoto.com: pages 14 (bottom), 27 (middle)
Photos.com: page 15 (top right)
Shutterstock.com: cover, pages 1 (girl and totem pole), 3, 4, 5 (except bottom right), 6, 7, 8 (background and bottom), 9, 10, 11, 12, 13, 14 (top), 15 (top left and bottom), 16, 17 (except bottom right), 18, 19 (except bottom), 20, 21, 22, 23 (except bottom left), 25, 26, 27 (top and bottom), 28, 29, 30
Other images by Circa Art and Object Gear

Library and Archives Canada Cataloguing in Publication

Kalman, Bobbie, 1947-
    What is culture? / Bobbie Kalman.

(Our multicultural world)
Includes index.
ISBN 978-0-7787-4635-5 (bound).--ISBN 978-0-7787-4650-8 (pbk.)

    1. Culture--Juvenile literature. I. Title. II. Series: Our multicultural world

GN357.K34 2009   j306   C2009-900486-0

Library of Congress Cataloging-in-Publication Data

Kalman, Bobbie.
    What is culture? / Bobbie Kalman.
        p. cm. -- (Our multicultural world)
    Includes index.
    ISBN 978-0-7787-4650-8 (pbk. : alk. paper) -- ISBN 978-0-7787-4635-5 (reinforced library binding : alk. paper)
    1. Culture--Juvenile literature. I. Title. II. Series.

GN357.K35 2009
306--dc22

2009002054

Crabtree Publishing Company

www.crabtreebooks.com   1-800-387-7650

Printed in the USA/082010/LG20100604

Published in Canada
Crabtree Publishing
616 Welland Ave.
St. Catharines, Ontario
L2M 5V6

Published in the United States
Crabtree Publishing
PMB 59051
350 Fifth Avenue, 59th Floor
New York, New York 10118

Published in the United Kingdom
Crabtree Publishing
Maritime House
Basin Road North, Hove
BN41 1WR

Published in Australia
Crabtree Publishing
386 Mt. Alexander Rd.
Ascot Vale (Melbourne)
VIC 3032

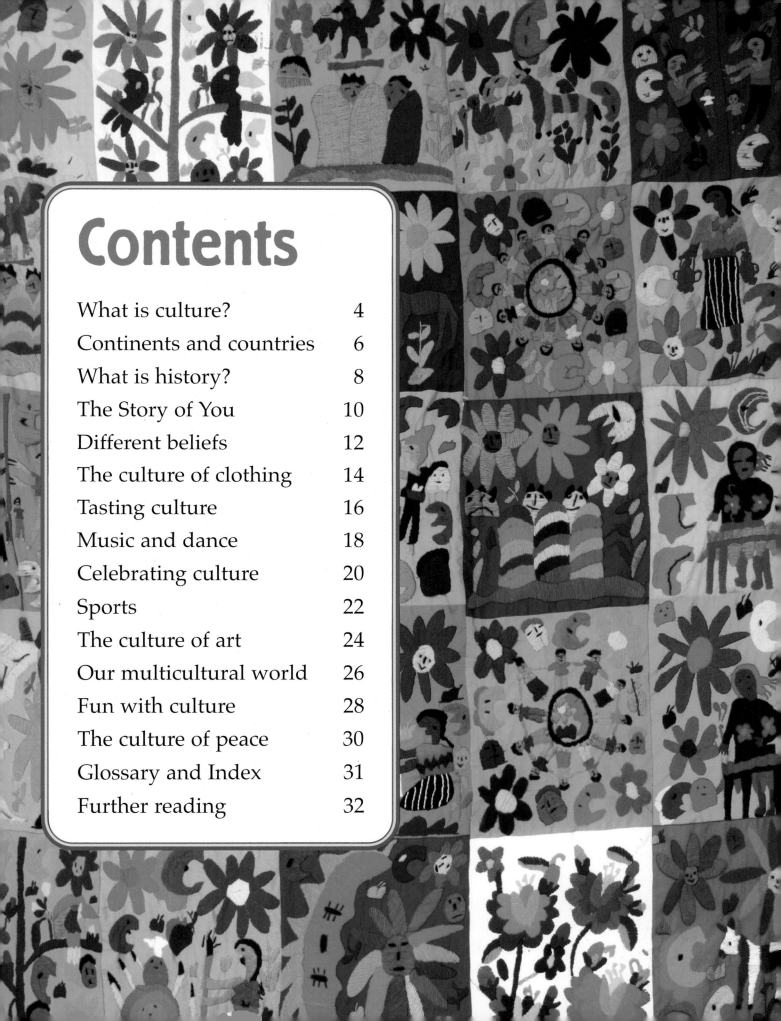

Contents

What is culture?	4
Continents and countries	6
What is history?	8
The Story of You	10
Different beliefs	12
The culture of clothing	14
Tasting culture	16
Music and dance	18
Celebrating culture	20
Sports	22
The culture of art	24
Our multicultural world	26
Fun with culture	28
The culture of peace	30
Glossary and Index	31
Further reading	32

What is culture?

Culture is the way we live. It is the clothes we wear, the foods we eat, the languages we speak, the stories we tell, and the ways we celebrate. It is the way we show our imaginations through art, music, and writing. Culture is also about our roots. Where did our **ancestors** come from? Ancestors are the people in our families who were alive long before we were. What do we believe? What makes our lives different from the lives of others? Come celebrate culture with us!

Culture is about our family stories. These boys are wearing African-style shirts. Their ancestors lived in Africa hundreds of years ago.

Culture is what, when, where, why, and how people celebrate. This Mexican boy is breaking a piñata at his birthday party. It is filled with candy.

People live all over the world. The people in each **country** have different ways of life. The pictures below show some of the things that make up the cultures on Earth.

music and dance

art

food

beliefs

history

clothing

sports

celebrations

Continents and countries

There are seven **continents** on Earth. Continents are huge areas of land. Most continents are made up of several countries. The people in each country speak different languages and have different cultures. Long ago, people did not know about one another's cultures. Now, people travel all over the world. They also **emigrate**, or leave their countries, to live in new countries.

This boy speaks two languages. He is reading a book that has words in English and Malay.

Countries have flags. This boy is holding an Australian flag.

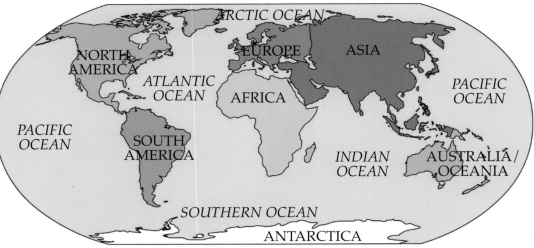

From largest to smallest, the continents are Asia, Africa, North America, South America, Antarctica, Europe, and Australia and Oceania.

*Antarctica is a cold place with many penguins and very few people. Most of the people who live there are **scientists**.*

Quebec City is in Canada. Canada is the biggest country in North America. Most of the people in Quebec City speak French.

Machu Picchu is in Peru. Peru is a country in South America. Machu Picchu was a city built more than 500 years ago by people called Incas.

This church is in Moscow, Russia's capital city. Russia is the biggest country in the world. It is in both Asia and Europe. Moscow is in Europe.

The Masai people live in Kenya, Africa. They move from place to place to feed their cattle, the way their ancestors did.

What is history?

History is a record of how people lived in the **past**. The past is the time before now. History is the stories of different cultures.

Stories told out loud

Some stories in history were told by grandparents to their grandchildren, who then shared them with their grandchildren. All around the world, Native peoples have passed down their histories **orally**, or through spoken words.

Books, movies, art

Histories are also found in books. Some history books describe events such as wars. Others show history through the writings and actions of people who lived during certain times. History can also be seen in paintings, statues, and buildings. History comes alive in festivals, celebrations, and in movies. What are your favorite ways to learn about history?

Native North American peoples told their histories through spoken stories.

Learning about a country's heroes helps us understand how people can change history.

Visiting historic villages, such as this **pioneer** village, is a great way to learn about history. History comes alive in the old shops and homes. People dressed in costumes work the way the pioneers did.

Children and adults love stories and movies about the pirates of long ago. There are many festivals today that celebrate pirates with costumes, parades, and fun activities. This boy is enjoying his day as a pirate.

Dressing in a historic costume can make you feel like a part of history, too.

The Story of You

History helps you learn about yourself. Who are you, and why do you live the way you live? The best place to start learning about history is to find out about your family. Where were you born? Where were your parents, grandparents, and ancestors born? Are both your parents from the same country and culture? You can learn a lot about yourself by writing a family history. Nothing is more fun—or more important—than writing the Story of You!

From which countries did your ancestors come? Find the countries on a map or globe.

Are your parents from the same country or culture? How many languages do you speak?

Learn more about the history of your ancestors from the Internet. Are you named after any famous people?

Ask your grandparents to show you pictures and tell you stories about their lives at your age. Make a list of all the ways your life is the same as theirs and how it is different.

What special **traditions** does your family have? Traditions are customs and beliefs passed down through families or cultures. This grandmother and her granddaughter are sharing a Thanksgiving recipe.

Share your story with other members of your family. It is their story, too!

Different beliefs

These girls are reading the Bible. The Bible is the holy book of Christianity.

A **religion** is a belief in a God or gods or in special ways that help people live better lives. Most religions have houses of worship, where people gather to practice their **faiths**, or beliefs. They also have holy books that contain the writings of religious leaders and teachers. Most religions have one or more **symbols**. Below are some religious symbols.

The cross is the symbol of Christianity. Christians believe that Jesus Christ is the son of God. Jesus died on a cross.

The crescent moon and star are part of the flags of some Islamic countries. Not all Muslims accept this symbol, however, because it was not used when Islam first became a religion.

The Star of David and the menorah are both symbols of Judaism. The star of David appears on the flag of Israel. The menorah is a symbol of the Jewish faith.

*Hindus chant the word "Om" when they **meditate**, or sit in silence. Hindus believe that "Om" is the sound from which Earth was created.*

The eight parts on this wheel represent the eight ways that Buddhists believe they can find peace and true happiness.

This Jewish boy is praying at the Western Wall in Jerusalem, Israel. He is reading from the Bible, which is written in the Hebrew language.

These Muslim girls are reading the Qur'an, the holy book of Islam. Muslims believe in one God, whose name is Allah in Arabic.

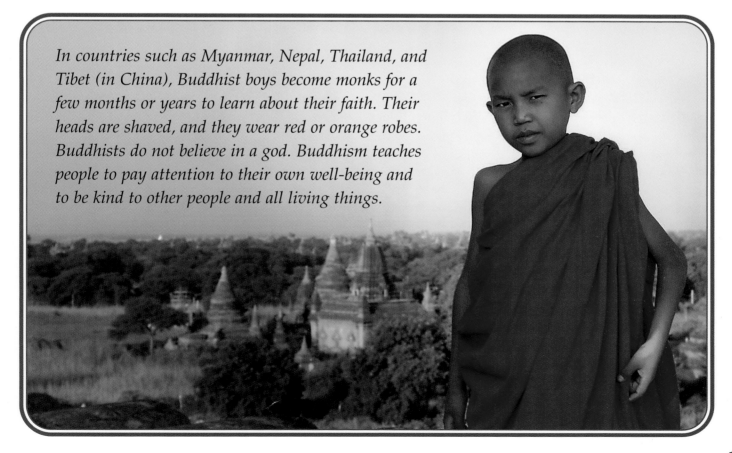

In countries such as Myanmar, Nepal, Thailand, and Tibet (in China), Buddhist boys become monks for a few months or years to learn about their faith. Their heads are shaved, and they wear red or orange robes. Buddhists do not believe in a god. Buddhism teaches people to pay attention to their own well-being and to be kind to other people and all living things.

The culture of clothing

Most children around the world wear modern clothes, like the clothes you wear. Some children also wear traditional clothes at special times, such as on holidays, at weddings, or during festivals. Sometimes older people in a family wear traditional clothing, whereas the children wear modern clothes. The young South Asian woman on the left is wearing traditional clothing, jewelry, and makeup on her wedding day. The boy on the right is wearing a traditional Korean suit.

Most children wear comfortable modern clothing. Jeans and T-shirts are favorite everyday outfits.

These children are dressed in traditional Indian jackets at a family party.

This Japanese grandmother is wearing a **kimono**. The rest of the family is dressed in modern clothes.

These Muslim boys live in Indonesia. They are wearing long, loose shirts and have caps on their heads. Many Muslim boys and girls keep their heads covered most of the time.

Tasting culture

Pizza came from Naples, Italy.

Food is a good way to learn about the cultures of others. Every time you eat food, you are tasting culture. Many of the foods you eat have come from other places. What are your favorite foods? Where were the foods first eaten?

Japanese sushi

Chinese fried rice

These children are eating Japanese food. They are using chopsticks.

Chunks of meat on **skewers**, or long sticks, are eaten in many countries, such as Greece and Thailand.

Curries are made in India and in many other countries in Asia. This curry is made with chicken and rice. The name "curry" comes from a mixture of spices.

Wrap sandwiches like these were made in Greece and Mexico. They are now eaten everywhere!

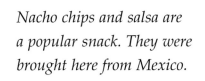

The first hamburger was served in the United States in 1902. Today, it is a favorite food in almost every country.

Nacho chips and salsa are a popular snack. They were brought here from Mexico.

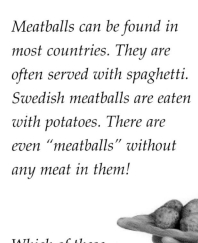

Meatballs can be found in most countries. They are often served with spaghetti. Swedish meatballs are eaten with potatoes. There are even "meatballs" without any meat in them!

Which of these delicious foods have you eaten? Which would you like to try?

Music and dance

Music and dancing make people feel happy. Most young people listen and dance to rock music. Each country also has traditional instruments, music, and dances that celebrate its cultures. Mexican *mariachi* music, for example, is played with guitars, violins, and trumpets. Accordion music is popular in many European countries such as Poland and Hungary.

accordion

guitar

These Chinese girls are dressed in red, the color that stands for happiness. They are singing and dancing in a group. Group dancing brings people together and teaches them to work as a team.

Get up and dance!

When people hear music, they want to dance. People dance in different ways. Some dances are difficult and are taught in dance schools. Some are made up or are learned from friends.

Ballet has difficult movements. This girl learned to dance at a ballet school.

ballet

breakdancing

Hip-hop dancing started on the streets of New York City. The first hip-hop dance was breakdancing.

Native and non-Native people meet to honor Native North American culture at events called powwows. Dancing is a big part of powwows. There are competitions in which Native dancers can show their skills.

Each Odissi dance movement has a meaning.

*Odissi dance is a very old **classical** Indian dance. Indian classical dance involves the mind and the body. Odissi dancing was first done in **temples** hundreds of years ago. Temples are houses of worship.*

Celebrating culture

lion dancer

To celebrate is to make an event special. People celebrate birthdays, religious holidays, and special times of the year. People also celebrate a country's history and heroes. They celebrate with music, dance, parades, costumes, and light. Food is a big part of most celebrations. What are your favorite celebrations? How do you celebrate these events?

People all over the world now celebrate festivals, such as Chinese New Year and the Lantern Festival, even if they are not Chinese!

Lions and dragons are a big part of these festivals. Lions stand for good luck, and dragons are a symbol of power.

The Lantern Festival ends the Chinese New Year. Bright lanterns are symbols of good luck and hope. Some lanterns are in the shapes of lions or dragons. Which animal shape is the lantern above?

menorah

Bumba Meu Boi is a popular festival in Northern Brazil. It takes place at the end of June. There are parades with dancers wearing fantastic costumes, such as these bird costumes.

The Jewish festival of Hanukkah lasts eight days. Each evening, a candle is lit on a menorah, and children receive gifts, money, or chocolate coins.

Both Americans and Canadians celebrate Thanksgiving, but at different times. A turkey meal is part of this family holiday. Turkey is also a favorite Christmas food in both countries.

Christmas is a Christian holiday that celebrates the birth of Jesus Christ. Santa Claus has become a part of Christmas. He is known by different names in many countries.

Sports

Sports are physical activities that are played by a set of rules. Some sports, such as running or skiing, can be done alone. Other sports are games played by two people or by teams. Many sports are played using balls. Soccer, football, tennis, and baseball are all ball games. Basketball was invented by a Canadian professor who nailed a peach basket to a wall and made up rules for playing the game.

peach basket

basketball

soccer ball

baseball

tennis

football

Football is an American game that is part rugby and part soccer.

Soccer is known as football in most countries. It is the most popular sport in the world. It was first played in England.

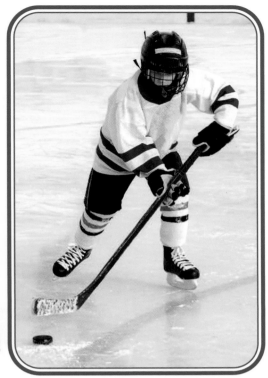

To play lacrosse, two teams try to score by passing and catching a ball using sticks with nets. Lacrosse was first played by Native North Americans almost a thousand years ago.

Hockey is the national winter sport of Canada. Hockey came from hockey-like games played by Scottish, Irish, and British immigrants.

Yoga is a great way to stretch the body and quiet the mind. Yoga came from India. It has been practiced there for over 5,000 years! Now, it is a popular exercise all over the world. Yoga means "union." Yoga helps bring together the body and mind.

Karate is a **martial art** that is part Japanese and part Chinese. Martial arts were created for self-defense. Karate moves include striking, punching, and kicking.

The culture of art

This picture is called "Carnation, Lily, Lily, Rose." It was painted by John Singer Sargeant, an American artist. It is his most popular work of art. What is your favorite work of art?

What is art?

Art is a way of using colors, shapes, and textures to create paintings, sculptures, or statues. Art can also be a beautiful dress, a play, a sport, or the way food is prepared. People show their imaginations and cultures through art.

The statue on the right is of Shiva, a Hindu god. It is a religious work of art and part of the culture of India.

This Korean boy's costume and kite are both works of art.

The picture on the left was created on a computer. It is made up of several photographs.

25

Our multicultural world

We live in a **multicultural** world. Multicultural means "made up of many cultures." People are different, but we are also the same. We are the same because we all need air, water, and food. We are the same because we all share the same home. Earth is our home. We are connected to one another because we live on Earth.

We are family!

People in a family are alike, but they are not the same. All over this world, people are different, too. We speak different languages, we sing different songs, we have different religions, and we show our imaginations in different ways. We have different talents and dreams. If we were all the same, Earth would be a boring place. The cultures in our world make Earth an exciting and fun place to live!

Diversity means variety.
Variety is colorful and fun.
Fun makes us feel free—
free to be different, you and me,
part of this big Earth family!

You have a whole world of sisters,
and a whole world of brothers, too.
Your Earth family is a wonderful thing.
Does it make you want to sing?

27

Fun with culture

Ask your teacher if your class or school can put on a culture fair. The fair could include foods from different countries, your family stories, works of art, a multicultural fashion show, music, and dancing. Each student can sign up for one or more events in the show. If you are a singer or dancer, you could teach a group of your friends a song or dance. If you love to cook, make some foods for everyone to enjoy! Your class can even create a **mural**, such as the one on the left, to decorate a wall in your classroom.

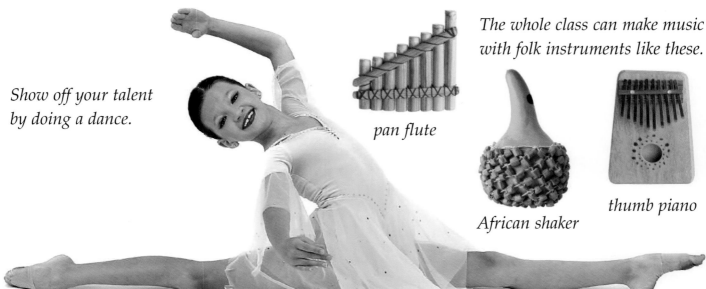

Show off your talent by doing a dance.

The whole class can make music with folk instruments like these.

pan flute

African shaker

thumb piano

Nothing is more fun than laughing! Dress like a clown, tell some jokes, and make people laugh out loud! Laughing is good for us all.

Put on a circus show. Teach your classmates how to juggle.

Learn about a special time in history and wear a costume from that time. Draw pictures and give a talk about how people lived in the past.

Do an exhibit of dolls from different countries.

Russian dolls

doll from Venice, Italy

The culture of peace

Do you have bad thoughts about others? Do you make fun of people because they do not look or dress like you do? Do you gossip about them behind their backs? Do you see differences as reasons for fighting? Do you hurt others? How would you feel if others did those things to you? Peace begins in our hearts and thoughts. We show it by our words and actions. Taking the vow of peace will change the world one person at a time. Will you take the vow?

Vow of peace

Put your hand over your heart. Think of someone you love and feel that love. With that loving feeling, promise to commit to peace in your thoughts, words, and actions. Say these words:

I promise to respect myself and others
in my thoughts, words, and actions.
I promise to treat others the way
I would like to be treated.
I know that peace begins with me.
Peace! Peace!
I am a child
of peace!

Glossary

Note: Some boldfaced words are defined where they appear in the book.

ancestor A relative of a person, who lived many years before that person

classical Describing a way of doing something in a traditional style

continent One of the seven large areas of land on Earth

country An area of land that has borders and a government

culture The way of life of a group of people

faith A belief or religion

history Stories or events from the past

kimono A loose robe that is tied at the waist

martial arts A type of sport that uses fighting skills for self-defense

mural A painting covering most of a wall

past Time that has gone by

pioneer First to explore or settle an area

scientist A person who studies science or works with it

symbol Something that stands for something else

tradition A set of beliefs or ways of doing things, which are passed down through families or culture groups

Index

ancestors 4, 7, 10, 11
art 4, 5, 8, 24–25, 28
beliefs 4, 5, 11, 12–13
books 6, 8, 12, 13
celebrations 4, 5, 8, 9, 20–21
clothing 4, 5, 14–15, 28
continents 6–7
costumes 9, 20, 21, 25, 29
countries 5, 6–7, 8, 9, 10, 12, 13, 17, 18, 20, 21, 22, 28, 29
dance 5, 18–19, 20, 21, 28
families 4, 10, 11, 14, 15, 21, 27, 28
festivals 8, 9, 14, 20–21
foods 4, 5, 16–17, 20, 21, 25, 26, 28
history 5, 8–9, 10, 11, 20, 29
languages 4, 6, 10, 13, 27
movies 8, 9
music 4, 5, 18, 19, 20, 28
Native Americans 8, 19, 23
parades 9, 20, 21
religion 12–13, 20, 25, 27
singing 18, 27, 28
sports 5, 22–23, 25
stories 4, 8, 9, 10, 11, 28
symbols 12, 20
traditions 11, 14, 15, 18

Further reading

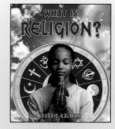

These books will help you learn more about culture: For more information about the books, look for them in your library or go to **www.crabtreebooks.com**.

Other books about culture in **Our Multicultural World** series: *What is Religion?; How are we the same and different?* Reading level: grades 3–4.

The Lands, Peoples, and Cultures series by **Bobbie Kalman**: Learn about the cultures and peoples who live in these countries: Afghanistan, Argentina, Australia, Brazil, Canada, China, Cuba, Egypt, El Salvador, England, France, Germany, Greece, India, Iran, Iraq, Ireland, Israel, Italy, Jamaica, Japan, Mexico, Nigeria, Pakistan, Peru, Philippines, Puerto Rico, Russia, South Africa, Spain, Sweden, and Vietnam. Reading level: grades 4–5.

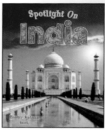

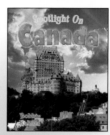
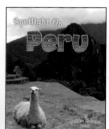

Multicultural Meals by **Bobbie Kalman** is full of delicious and healthy recipes from different countries. Making these yummy recipes will allow you to "taste" culture. Reading level: grade 3.

Spotlight On My Country series by **Bobbie Kalman**: This series is for younger readers. It includes these countries: Australia, Canada, China, Mexico, India, Peru, and the United States of America. Reading level: grades 2–3.

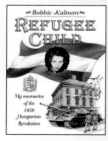

Refugee Child is the exciting story of author Bobbie Kalman's experiences during the Hungarian Revolution, her middle-of-the-night escape across the border to Austria, and her life as a refugee and immigrant. Bobbie overcame many obstacles on her way to becoming an author of hundreds of children's books. This book is multiculturalism in action! Reading level: grades 4–5.

Celebrations in My World series explores the history and traditions of major celebrations around the world, including: *Christmas, Easter, Chinese New Year, Day of the Dead, Earth Day, Halloween, Passover, Thanksgiving, Diwali, Cinco de Mayo, Ramadan, Hanukkah, Kwanzaa, Martin Luther King, Jr. Day,* and *Constitution Day.* Reading level: grades K–2.